Properties of Matter

by Emily Gray

PEARSON
Scott
Foresman

DK

Properties of Matter

Elements

Elements are the building blocks of matter. There are more than one hundred elements. It is very difficult to break elements down into different materials.

Elements combine in many ways to make up all the different kinds of matter around us. Only a few elements are found in pure forms in nature. Living and nonliving things are made up of arrangements of different elements.

Each element has its own set of chemical and physical properties. Groups of elements with similar physical and chemical properties are known as families.

silver ore

The metals gold and silver belong to the same family of elements. Metals come from rocks called ores.

chunks of gold ore in quartz crystals

old silver coin

old gold coin

The metal used to make this spring is shiny and bendable. These are its physical properties.

Chemical properties are the ways that matter changes. For example, liquid water has the chemical property that it can be broken down by electricity into oxygen gas and hydrogen gas. Physical properties can be measured without changing the material. An object's color, mass, volume, odor, texture, and density are all physical properties. These properties can be measured using tools such as rulers, microscopes, thermometers, and scales.

Elements are classified as either metals or nonmetals. More than three-fourths of all elements are metals. Some physical properties of metals are that they are shiny, they are bendable, and they can conduct heat and electricity well.

Nonmetals are often gases and do not conduct electricity. They may be transparent and are usually fragile.

iron ore

The metal element iron is often mixed with the nonmetal carbon to produce steel.

steel screw

Weight, Mass, and Volume

You can use scales to measure the weight of an object. Weight is the pull of gravity on an object. An object's weight can also be measured by adding up the weight of all of its parts. This is useful for objects that won't fit on a scale. The sum of the weights of the parts equals the weight of the entire object.

The pull of gravity is not the same everywhere on Earth. The weight of an object may be different if it is measured in two different places. At higher altitudes on Earth, gravity is weaker. An object weighed at the top of a mountain would weigh less than if it were weighed at sea level.

Mass is the amount of matter in an object. An object's mass affects its weight, but weight and mass are two different things.

Weight changes as the force of gravity changes, but mass stays the same. The mass of an object is usually measured using a balance. The object you are measuring is placed on one side, and other objects with known masses are placed on the other side. When both sides balance, youadd the known masses. The object's mass is equal to the total of the known masses. For example, if five grams of mass balance an object, that object's mass is five grams.

Use a balance to measure the mass of objects.

You can measure the volume of a piece of clay by dropping it into a container full of water. The amount of water that spills out into a measuring jug is the clay's volume.

Volume is the amount of space occupied by an object. The volume of a solid is measured in cubic units. To find the volume of a box, you can use a simple mathematical formula. Multiply the length, width, and height to find the volume.

But what if an object has a strange shape that is hard to measure, such as a lumpy piece of clay? The volume of such an object can be measured with a graduated cylinder, as shown above. When the lump of clay is placed in the jug of water, some of the water spills out through the straw. The water is collected in the graduated cylinder. The volume of water shown on the cylinder's markings is the same as the volume of the clay.

Properties of Objects and Materials

The properties of an object are not always the same as the properties of a material. For example, shape is a property of an object, not a property of the material from which the object is made. The density, color, hardness, and texture are properties of materials, not objects.

Density and Buoyancy

Density is the amount of matter in a specific volume. If you have a golf ball and a table tennis ball that are the same volume, but one has more mass, their densities are different. The density of an object can be calculated by dividing the mass of the object by the volume of the object. This equation can be written as $D = \dfrac{M}{V}$.

Density is a physical property. The density of a material does not change even if the size of the object does. For example, the density of a tiny sliver of glass is the same as the density of a huge windowpane.

Golf balls and table tennis balls may have about the same volume, but their densities are different because the golf ball has more mass.

If an object can float, it is buoyant. Objects with different buoyancies are used for different things. For example, life jackets and balloons are buoyant. They are designed to float. Anchors and lead weights are not buoyant. They are designed to sink. Certain materials are used for each purpose.

Buoyancy is the density of an object compared to the density of the material around it. For example, wood is less dense than water, so it floats in water. Wood is more dense than air, so it does not float in air.

A lemon floats in water, but if you peel the lemon, it will sink.

An unpeeled lemon is less dense than the surrounding water, so it floats.

A peeled lemon is more dense than water, so it sinks.

How do atoms combine?

Atoms

An **atom** is the smallest part of an element that has the chemical properties of that element. When two or more atoms combine, a molecule is formed. The atoms of elements can react with one another. They can combine to form chemical compounds in many different ways. The properties of an atom determine how atoms react and combine with one another. These properties also determine how elements react with other elements.

This diagram shows the structure of a carbon atom. At the center of the atom is the nucleus.

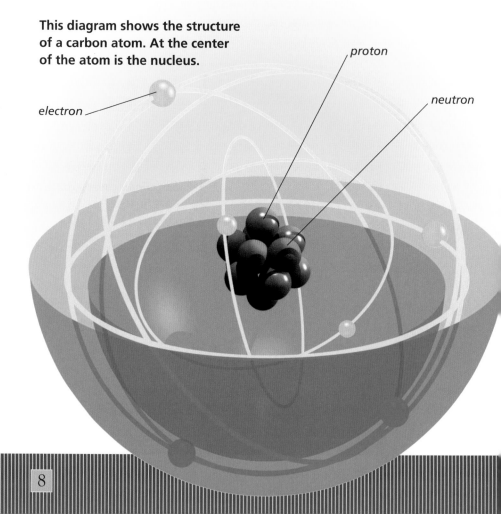

proton

neutron

electron

Atoms are made up of particles called electrons, protons, and neutrons. The nucleus, or center, of an atom consists of protons and neutrons. Each element has a unique number of protons. For example, an atom of carbon has six protons. No other element has this number of protons in its atoms. The nucleus is surrounded by electrons. Some particles have a property known as an electrical charge.

Neutrons have no electrical charge. **Electrons** have a negative charge, while **protons** have a positive charge. These charges react with one another as a magnet would: the negative charge and positive charge attract one another. This attraction holds the atom together. An atom usually has an equal number of protons and electrons. This makes the atom electrically neutral, which means that the negative and positive charges are equal.

All elements are recorded in a chart known as the periodic table. Every element has a box in the table that shows the name of the element and its symbol. The symbol has one, two, or three letters. The first letter of the symbol is capitalized. The box also contains the atomic number, which is the number of protons in the nucleus.

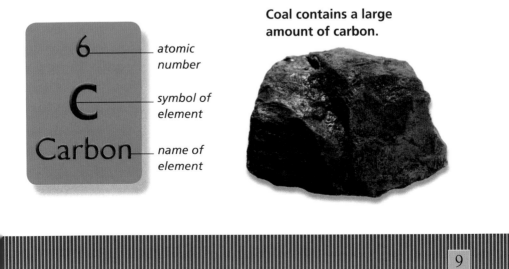

6 — atomic number

C — symbol of element

Carbon — name of element

Coal contains a large amount of carbon.

Compounds

A **compound** is a type of matter made up of two or more elements. Compounds act differently than the elements they are made up of. For example, water is a compound made up of hydrogen and oxygen. Both of these elements are gases at room temperature. But water is a liquid.

A water molecule is made up of two atoms of hydrogen and one atom of oxygen.

Some compounds hold together because they share electrons. The electrons go around two atoms, bonding the atoms together.

Each compound can be described using a formula. The formula tells how many atoms of each element are in the compound. The formula for water is H_2O. The 2 after the H means that there are two hydrogen atoms in one molecule of water. There is no number after the O. This means there is only one oxygen atom per water molecule. A molecule is the smallest particle of a compound.

formula for water

symbol for oxygen

symbol for hydrogen

This means that there are two hydrogen atoms in one molecule of water.

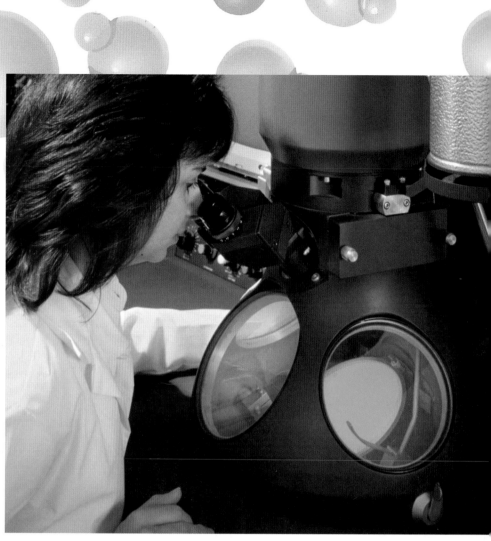

This machine helps scientists to see things that are too small to be seen with a regular microscope.

Seeing Molecules

Molecules and atoms are too small to be seen. Even the most powerful microscope cannot help you see an atom or molecule. In order to make images of atoms and molecules, special technology is needed. Scientists use powerful equipment to detect the shape of an atom or a molecule. Then the shape is shown on a computer screen.

Salts

Salts are compounds that bond in a certain way. The elements in salts are held together by opposite charges, like magnets. If an atom has more electrons than protons, it has a negative charge. An atom with more protons than electrons has a positive charge.

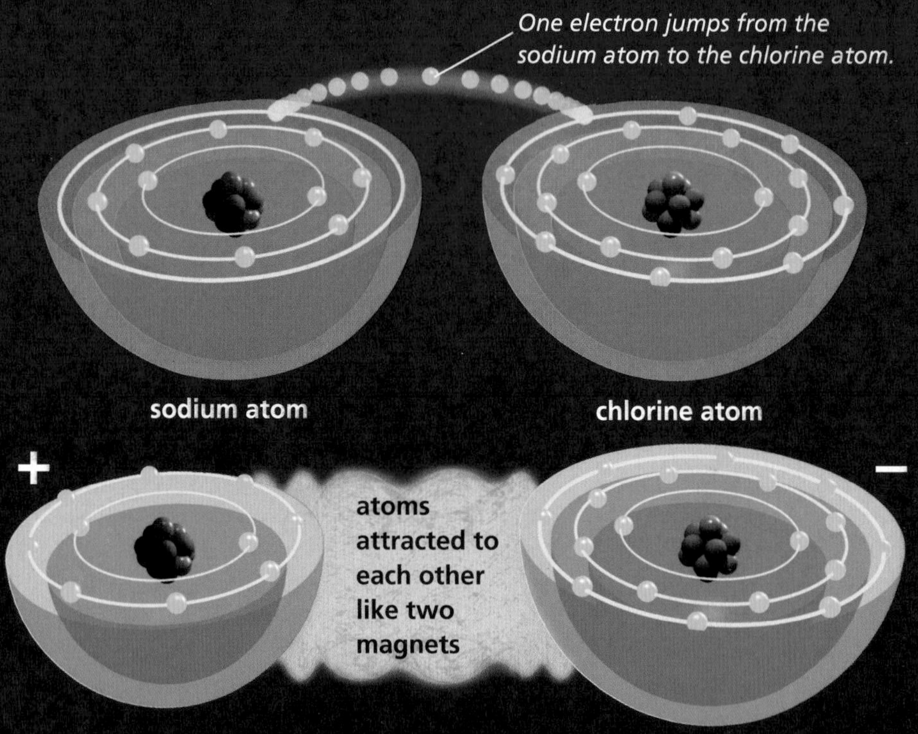

One electron jumps from the sodium atom to the chlorine atom.

sodium atom   chlorine atom

+   −

atoms
attracted to
each other
like two
magnets

The sodium atom now has more protons than electrons. This gives the atom a positive charge.

The chlorine atom now has more electrons than protons. This gives the atom a negative charge.

lar pattern of atoms
crystals

chlorine atom

made up of one metal element and c
ement. All salts form crystals. This m
olecules are arranged in a repeating p
usually brittle, and they have high m
er crystals include sand, sugar, and di
earned, compounds are very differen
s that combine to make them. Salt is
One molecule of table salt is made up
sodium (Na) and one atom of chlor
for table salt is written as NaCl. Pur
at is soft and silver. Pure chlorine is a
s. Separately, these elements can be h
, they form a compound that is safe t

Phase Changes

Solids and Liquids

There are three phases, or states, of matter. Matter may be a solid, a liquid, or a gas. The motions and arrangements of atoms and molecules, along with the temperature of the material, determine the state of the material. For example, water is in a solid state when it freezes and becomes ice. We can drink water in its liquid state, at room temperature. When water is found in the air, it is a gas. These states are considered physical properties and do not depend on chemical reactions.

Solids have a fixed shape and volume. Their particles vibrate in place. Strong forces hold the particles together.

When the temperature rises, molecules can gain enough energy to move away from their positions. Then the solid melts and turns into a liquid. Molecules in a liquid are still held together, but they are not in a fixed position. They can move past and around one another. Although liquids do not have a definite shape, they still have a fixed volume.

Ice is water in a solid state.

Particles in a solid are tightly packed.

Particles in a liquid have space to move around.

As the temperature drops, liquids eventually freeze. The molecules and atoms slow down and vibrate in place again. A material's melting temperature is always the same as its freezing temperature. For example, when the temperature of water in liquid form cools below 0° Celsius, it freezes into ice. When the temperature of ice rises above 0° Celsius, it turns from a solid to a liquid. The temperature at which this change occurs is known as the melting point or the freezing point.

The freezing point is not the same for all materials. You can determine what a material is by its freezing point, because different materials have different freezing points.

The freezing point of a material is a physical property, because nothing is added to or subtracted from the material during the change. Only the temperature of the material changes.

Water is in a liquid state at room temperature.

When water reaches its boiling point, it becomes a gas. The steam erupting from this geyser is a gas.

Particles in a gas are widely spaced and move around freely.

Gases

Gas particles are very far apart compared to the particles of solids or liquids. A gas does not have a fixed shape or volume. Gas particles spread out evenly to fill a container. Gas particles usually do not affect each other unless they collide, because they are far apart.

Evaporation happens when liquids turn into gas. Particles at the surface of a liquid evaporate if they move upward with enough speed.

If the temperature of a liquid is high enough, particles will evaporate throughout the liquid. This is called boiling. The bubbles in boiling water are gas that has evaporated below the surface and is rising to the top.

Different types of matter have different melting points. The same holds true for the boiling point of a substance. The boiling point is the temperature at which a liquid changes to a gas. Different liquids have different boiling points. The boiling point of a liquid is a physical property. Nothing is added to or subtracted from a substance when it boils.

The boiling point is not always a fixed temperature. The boiling point of a substance is sensitive to changes in pressure. If you boiled water at sea level, the boiling point would be slightly higher than if you were to boil the same water on a high mountain. This temperature difference is not large but has been recorded by scientists.

Condensation occurs when a gas turns back into a liquid. If gas particles touch a cold surface, their temperature drops. As they cool, they slow down and become trapped on the surface. If enough atoms are trapped, a liquid drop is formed. The clouds we see in the sky form by condensation of water.

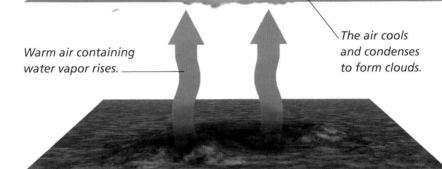

The air cools and condenses to form clouds.

Warm air containing water vapor rises.

When water condenses in the atmosphere, it forms clouds.

Mixtures and Solutions

Mixtures

When different materials are put together but do not form compounds, a mixture is formed. Usually, the materials keep their distinct properties. For example, if you mix lettuce, tomatoes, and peppers together in a salad, the colors and flavors of each vegetable do not change.

Materials in simple mixtures can be separated if they have different physical properties. For example, iron filings and sand can be separated easily with a magnet. The iron filings are attracted to the magnet, while the grains of sand are not. Moving a magnet over this mixture will pick up the iron filings, leaving the sand behind.

A mixture of iron filings and sand can be separated easily with a magnet. The iron sticks to the magnet, leaving the sand behind.

Brass is an alloy of copper and zinc. Neither copper nor zinc is strong enough to make a bell, but brass is.

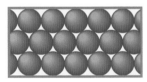

Atoms in a metal element are arranged in a regular pattern.

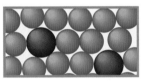

Atoms in an alloy are arranged in an irregular pattern. This makes the metal stronger.

Some common metals are elements, while others are mixtures of elements. Gold, silver, copper, iron, and nickel are all examples of metals that are elements. Steel is a mixture of iron and carbon, while brass is a mixture of copper and zinc. Bronze is another example of a mixture. It is made up of tin, copper, and several other materials. All of these mixtures are known as alloys. The properties of an alloy are usually different than the properties of the materials used to make the alloy.

A few sugar crystals have not dissolved.

These pieces of chalk do not form a solution with water.

Sugar crystals do form a solution with water.

Solutions

Solutions are special mixtures of two or more substances. Solutions are different from mixtures. If you make a mixture of dirt and water, the dirt will eventually sink to the bottom. If you mix sugar and water, the sugar will dissolve in the water and will not sink to the bottom. This combination of sugar and water is an example of a solution. In a solution, substances are spread out evenly. They will not settle out as the dirt did in the water.

Solutions form when molecules have attractions for one another. These electrical charges hold molecules together and also allow liquids to dissolve other substances. The substance that dissolves in the liquid is known as a solute. The liquid in which a solute dissolves is known as a solvent.

Solvents can dissolve solutes only if the molecules of each substance have similar attractive forces. Water is called a universal solvent because it can act as a solvent in many different solutions. Sugar, starch, and salt all dissolve in water.

When a solute dissolves in a solvent, the individual particles of the solute separate and spread throughout the solvent. Solids can dissolve in a liquid more quickly if the pieces are smaller.

Salt water is a solution of salt dissolved in water. The two materials can be separated by evaporating the water.

Collect the water droplets in a bowl. The salt will remain in the pan.

Boil the solution in a pan with a lid. The water evaporates and then condenses on the lid.

When the mixture of chalk and water is heated, the chalk still does not dissolve in the water.

When the solution of sugar and water is heated, the remaining sugar crystals dissolve.

Heating a solution can also increase the rate at which liquids and solids dissolve in each other. When materials are heated, their particles spread out. This helps the solute dissolve faster in the solvent.

Not all solutions are composed of a solid and a liquid. Solutions can be made when liquids dissolve into other liquids. A gas can also dissolve into a liquid. Oceans contain dissolved salt, which is a solid. Oceans also contain dissolved oxygen and carbon dioxide, which are gases. These substances help the ocean to sustain plant and animal life.

Solubility is the amount of a substance that can be dissolved by a solvent at a specific temperature. Solid solutes can be dissolved in solutions with higher temperatures.

Solutions can be described by how much solute is dissolved in the solvent. **Saturated** solutions contain all the solute that can be dissolved in the solution. If you add more solute to a saturated solution, it will not dissolve unless you raise the temperature. A solution is **concentrated** when it has so much solute that it is close to being saturated. A **dilute** solution contains only a small amount of solute.

Some materials will not dissolve in a liquid at all. Raising the temperature or changing the proportions of the solute to solvent will not help. Although salt will dissolve easily in water, salt cannot dissolve in oil.

Pour oil on top of water and add a droplet of food coloring. What happens when you stir the mixture?

oil

food coloring

water

The oil does not form a solution with the coloring or the water.

The coloring and water will form a solution.

Glossary

atom   the smallest part of an element that has the properties of the element

compound   a substance created with two or more elements that has different properties than the elements

concentrated   a state in which a solvent contains a large amount of dissolved solute

dilute   a state in which a solvent contains a small amount of dissolved solute

electron   a negatively charged particle of an atom

element   matter that cannot be easily broken down into simpler substances

neutron   a particle of an atom with no charge

proton   a positively charged particle of an atom

saturated   a state in which a solvent contains all of the solute that can be dissolved in it

What did you learn?

1. Why are elements the "building blocks of matter"?

2. Mass, volume, and density are words used to describe three different properties of matter. Explain each term.

3. What are the particles that make up an atom? Name the charge each particle has.

4. **Writing** in Science Mixtures and solutions both combine materials. Write to explain how mixtures and solutions are different, and give an example from the text for each to support your answer.

5. **Predict** Weight is the pull of gravity on an object. What do you think would happen to an object's weight if there were no gravity at all?

Science

Genre	Comprehension Skill	Text Features	Science Content
Nonfiction	Predict	• Labels • Captions • Diagrams • Glossary	Matter

Scott Foresman Science 5.11

scottforesman.com

ISBN 0-328-13947-5

9 780328 139477

90000

THE
EARTH
and Its Neighbors

by Donna Latham

Vocabulary

asteroid
axis
comet
Moon phase
revolution
rotation
satellite
solar system
space probe

ISBN: 0-328-13965-3